SUPER Dinky Doodles

I'm Doolila, Doodle Monster's girlfriend!

And I'm Doodle Monster. Look out for us inside!

priddy books
big ideas for little people

Fill the page
with tiny happy
hearts!

Use your
stickers!

Give this tree a big trunk!

what is Doodle Monster drawing?

Give this apple a face!

Crunch! Munch!

Use your stickers!

Complete the doodle lines, then start your own!

Do you dare fill this page with squares?

Give these teddy bears cuddly bodies!

Doodle a face around these googly eyes!

Doodle more spacecraft in outer space!

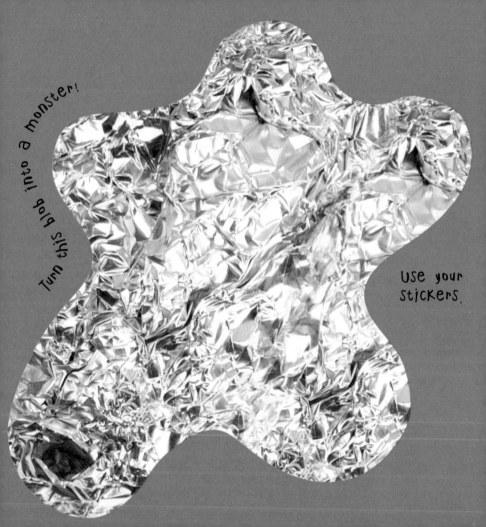

Turn this blob into a monster!

Use your stickers.

Complete the
dotty pattern.

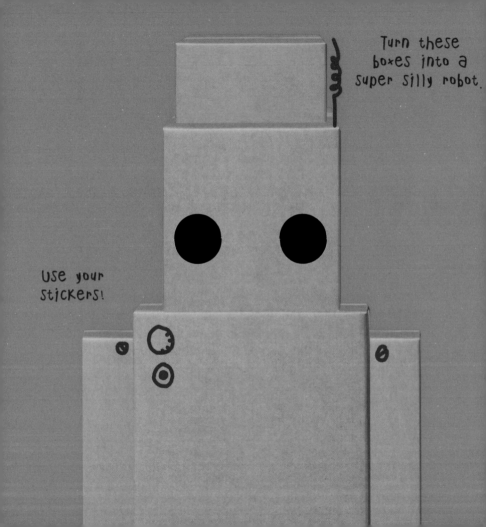

Give him a super long tongue.

Ah!

Doodle a lily pad for the frog to sit on.

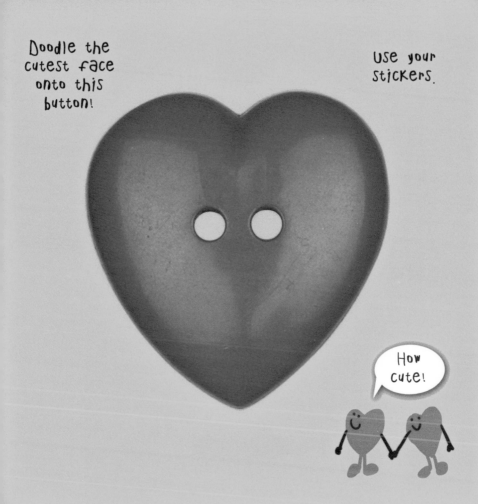

Tom the Tomato needs a smiley face!

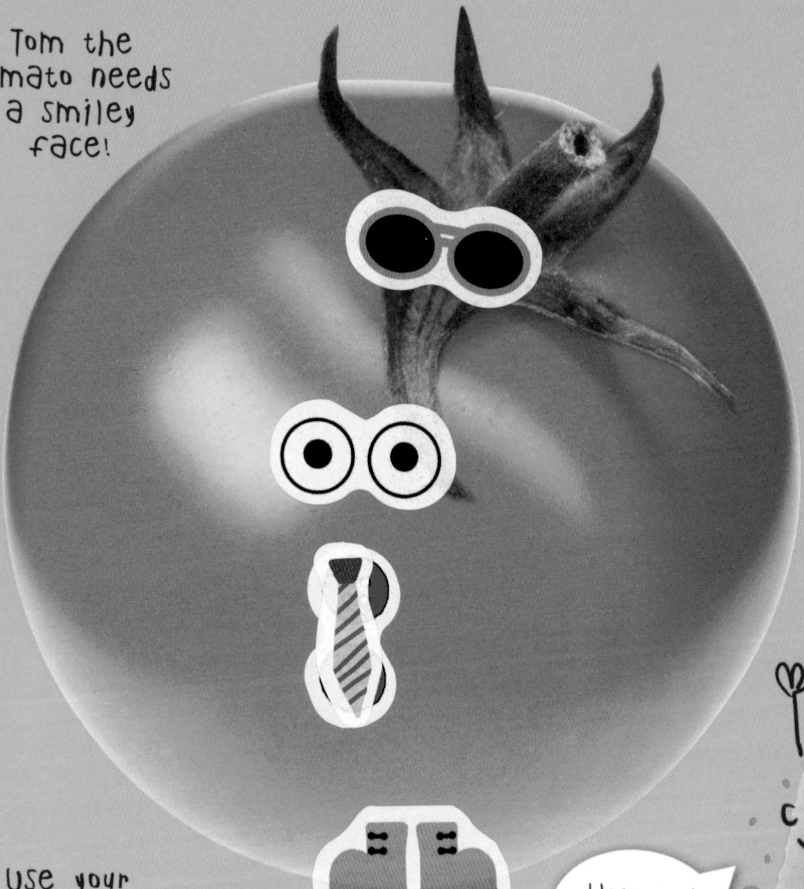

Use your stickers.

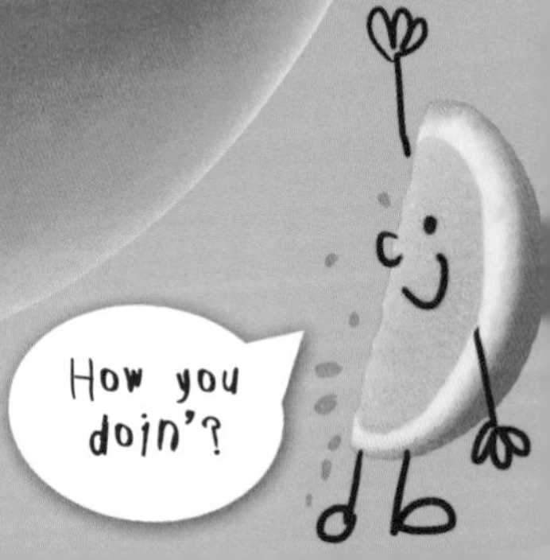

Complete
the wiggly
pattern!

Fill this page with rectangles!

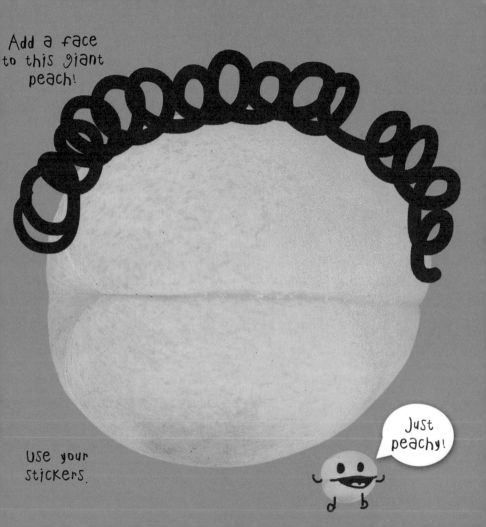

Add a face to this giant peach!

Use your stickers.

Just peachy!

Doodle the owner of these funky purple sunglasses.

Like me!

Fill the frames with your favorite things!

Doodle the owner of these pretty eyes.

Draw in the rest of this shoal of fish.

Under the sea!

Add more treats to this giant cookie!

Hmm, looking good!

Doodle dots on all the other dice!

Turn these paint splats
into creatures.

Bonjour!

Draw other animal faces on these apples.

Ah! A giant mouse!

Fill the basket with puppies!

Doodle your dream house into this house shape.

Add doodles and patterns to the paint palette!

Give this seriously stylish starfruit a face!

Bonjour!
Good day!

Use your
stickers!

Make Doodle Monster smile!

Make
Doolila smile!

Doodle vacation things on top of the camper van.

Complete this page by adding more
and more squares!

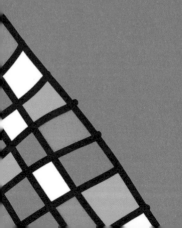

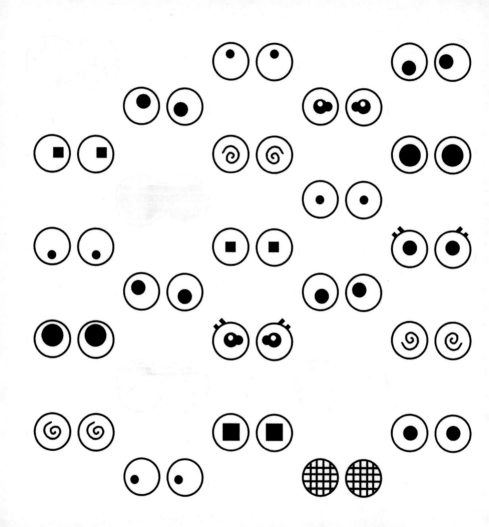

Doodle the rest of the town. Honk!

I'm a
fried egg!

Create some creatures
with features!

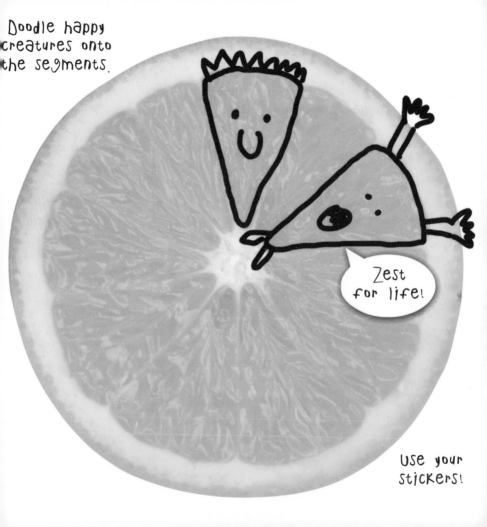

who is riding in this cool car?

Doodle them in the front seats.

Treasure!

Add more fish to this underwater scene.

Turn this face into a giant happy star!

Give the sleepy Moon a snuggly hat for bedtime.

It wasn't me!

Fill this page with lots of paint splotches and splats!

Complete the colorful patterns.

Design your
own family
crest!

Use your
stickers!

Star man!

Turn these shapes into little people!

where's 8, my mate?

Create some cool-looking numbers!

Turn these fingerprints into animals.

what are Doodle Monster and Doolila looking at?

what a
view!

Add more chocolate block buildings and people!

Doodle lots of birds in the sky to make a flock!

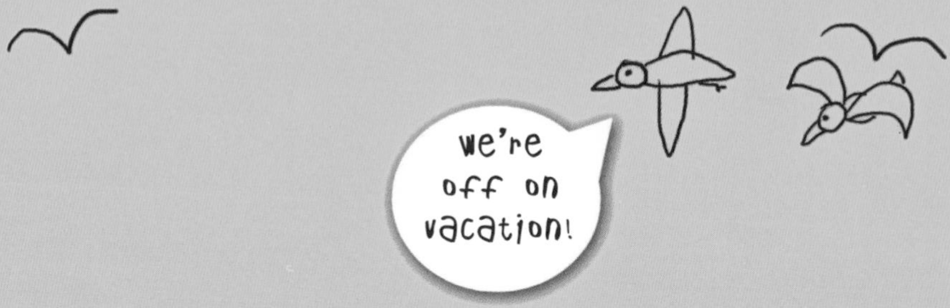

what has just hatched out of the egg?

Doodle the
owner of
these eyes.

Turn these boxes into scary creatures.

ROAR!

Doodle a picture of your favorite animal.

Continue the paint blotch and fill the page.

Pink, scary, and hairy!

Turn this hairy pink fluff into a monster!

who is holding on to the heart-shaped balloons?

Turn these hearts into little people.

Complete the spiral pattern and fill up the page.

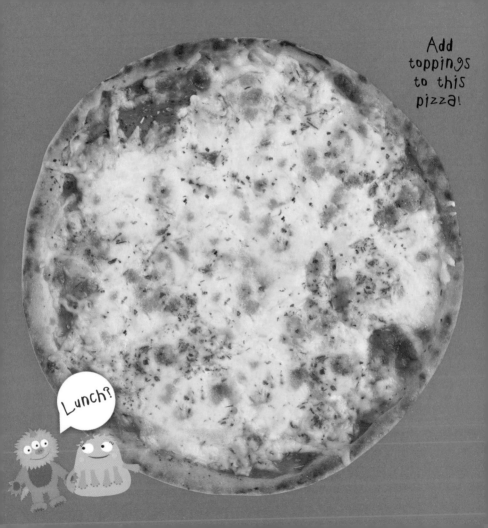

what will you doodle on this note?

use your stickers!

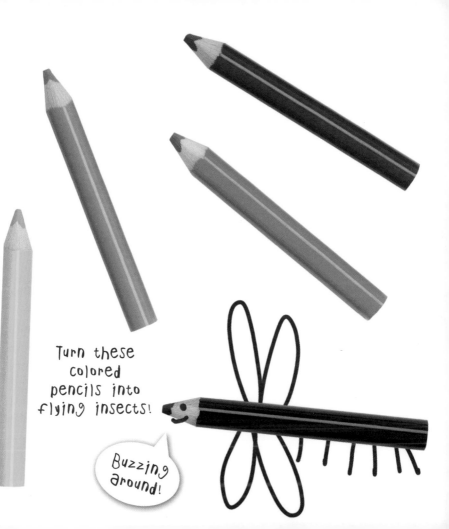

Turn these colored pencils into flying insects!

Buzzing around!

Give Ted a smiley, cuddly face.

Give this crazy banana a face.

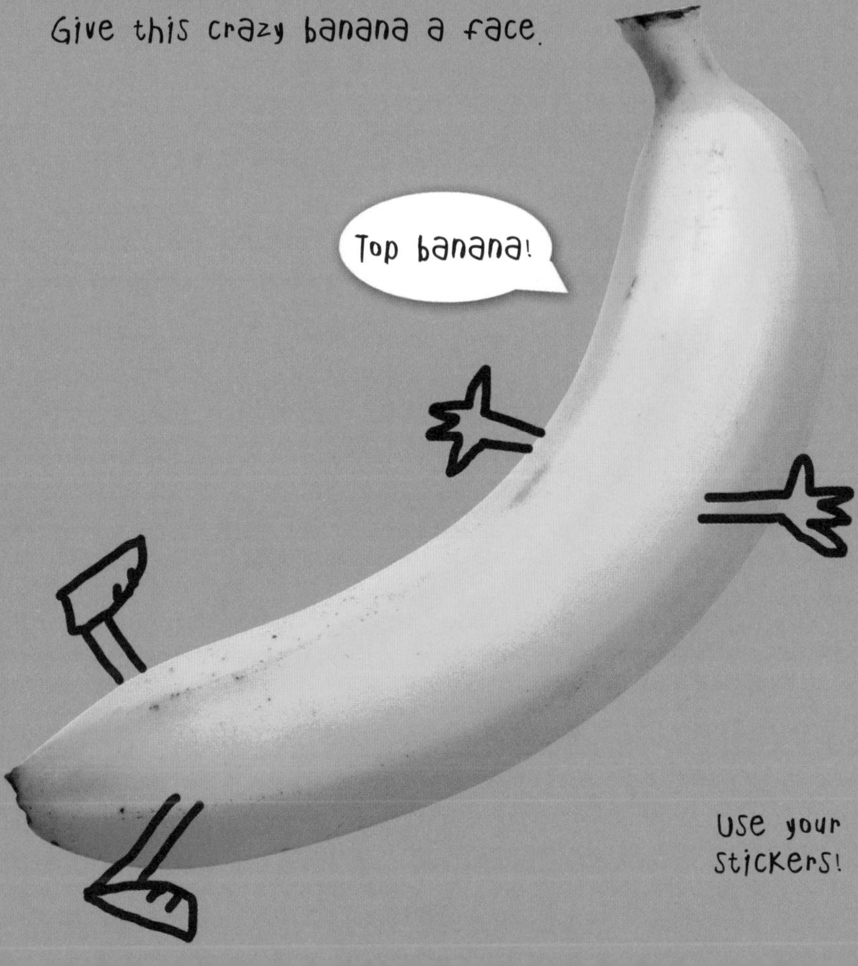

Use your stickers!

Doodle more lightning bolts shooting from this angry cloud.

Fill the page with bumpy lines.

Fill the page with zigzag lines.

Add faces to the cereal!

Fill the page with more paw prints!

Fill up the dump truck with rocks and dirt!

Doodle what this camel
is thinking about.